Healing Words

Healing Words

*Includes the original words
of Kathryn Kuhlman*

Larry Keefauver, editor

CREATION
HOUSE
Orlando, FL

Published by Creation House
Strang Communications Company
600 Rinehart Road
Lake Mary, FL 32746
Phone: 407-333-3132
Fax: 407-333-7100
Web site: http://www.creationhouse.com

All Scripture quotations are from the King James Version of the Bible.

Interior design by Lillian McAnally

Copyright © 1997 by Creation House
All rights reserved
Printed in the United States of America
Library of Congress Catalog Card Number: 96-71920
International Standard Book Number: 0-88419-460-4

78901234 BVG 87654321

To my first love, Jesus Christ, and to His glory
for saving and healing scores of people through
the ministry of Kathryn Kuhlman.
—Larry Keefauver

"By His Stripes, we are healed!"

Contents

❧

Foreword

HAVE YOU BEEN WAITING FOR ME?"

Absolutely!

The whole world was waiting to hear the flaming redhead from Concordia, Missouri. On the waiting list were Hollywood movie stars, presidents, and kings—even the Pope.

Kathryn Kuhlman with the familiar raspy voice, slow speech, and folksy sermons became a household name to millions in the media.

The late Dr. C. M. Ward, a longtime friend of mine, predicted in the latter fifties that two significant changes were ahead for the church. First, there would be an exploding emphasis on Bible teaching. Second, it was time in history for a powerful female personality to emerge with a ministry of the miraculous.

The moment I heard Dr. Ward's forecast, I sensed that this divinely designed lady-in-waiting could be none other than Miss Kathryn Kuhlman.

When I invited Kathryn Kuhlman to minister in Southern California, she was hesitant. There must be a clear confirmation that it was God's will and timing. She would pray. Finally, on the third day, Miss Kuhlman told my wife, who was visiting in her home, that she now felt a release to add California to the ministry base.

Soon a door opened at CBS television. Turn-away crowds jammed every meeting. Eternity alone will record the numbers of those miraculously healed and born again in a ministry that circled the globe.

As you read these daily devotions, remember that you are studying carefully documented, treasured teachings of the late Kathryn Kuhlman. The material is based on and includes actual word-for-word statements taken from her sermons on audiotape and video.

A library containing the entire collection of Kathryn Kuhlman videos—with the exception of one—is available through Beyond Productions. All of the videos in the Classic Library are live services conducted by Miss Kuhlman.

Dr. Ralph Wilkerson
April 1997

Introduction

A S A FOURTEEN-YEAR-OLD GIRL, Kathryn Kuhlman began her remarkable relationship with Jesus Christ in a little Methodist church nestled in Concordia, Missouri. In the coming pages you will read of her conversion and her first experience with the baptism of the Holy Spirit.

Kathryn dropped out of high school at the age of seventeen to travel with her sister and brother-in-law, Myrtle and Everett Parrott, on a tent-meeting circuit during the summer of 1924.

The Parrotts schooled Kathryn in the basics of ministry—evangelism, preaching, faith healing and Pentecostalism. After a brief period of Bible school training, she and her sister Helen began to evangelize and preach in Oregon, Idaho, Montana, and Wyoming. In 1933 they traveled to Denver and began to hold large meetings in the Denver Revival Tabernacle.

In 1938 she married traveling evangelist, Burroughs Allen Waltrip, leaving the Tabernacle and establishing their ministry in Mason City, Iowa, at Radio Chapel. The ministry there, however, fell on hard financial times and faltered. The marriage was a painful period in Kathryn's life from 1938 until its dissolution in 1946. But her ministry would be renewed and experience new growth.

In 1946 Kathryn Kuhlman began a series of meetings in northwestern Pennsylvania at the Franklin Gospel Tabernacle. She later moved to a renovated skating rink, Faith Temple. She also started holding meetings in Pittsburgh at Carnegie Hall, saying she would stay there until the work was done. In 1950 she moved to Pittsburgh where her ministry was based for the rest of her life.

The crowds attending her services in Pittsburgh grew so large by the year of 1967 that she started the Friday night miracle services at First Presbyterian Church. She also conducted services in the surrounding areas, especially in Akron and Cleveland. But she did not venture beyond the friendly surroundings of Pennsylvania and Ohio.

In 1965 Pastor Ralph Wilkerson, who pastored at Melodyland in Anaheim, California, persuaded Kuhlman to conduct one meeting at his church. This opened the door for succeeding meetings not only in Southern California but in scores of other cities throughout the country. She began a television ministry for CBS, *I Believe in Miracles*. In the early seventies Kathryn appeared a number of times on the campus of Oral Roberts University to speak at chapel and graduation services.

In late 1975 Kathryn's doctors determined that she needed heart surgery. Following surgery in December, Kathryn struggled physically until February 20, 1976. She died and went home to meet the One she loved so dearly, Jesus.

This devotional book has been compiled from Kathryn Kuhlman's taped appearances at Oral Roberts University, audiotaped interviews at

Melodyland, and from the only miracle service she ever allowed to be filmed—at Melodyland in 1969. I want to acknowledge my deep appreciation to Ralph Wilkerson who has granted permission for us to transcribe and edit from these rare video appearances for this unique devotional book.

I first heard of Kathryn Kuhlman from two sources—my mother, who attended her services in Pittsburgh, and Benny Hinn, who mentions her often in his crusade ministry which, it can be argued, has been deeply influenced by Kathryn Kuhlman. While her ministry published a number of books about Kathryn Kuhlman and the healing stories that came out of her meetings, there are few resources that simply share her words about healing, faith, and her relationship with her One love—Jesus Christ.

Kathryn Kuhlman's appearance in her healing meetings was both dramatic and intensely personal. She paid the price of ministry, giving herself totally to the ministry of proclaiming the gospel and the healing power of Jesus Christ. The words she spoke went far beyond preaching and teaching. They ministered both comfort and healing to those who opened themselves to the power of the Holy Spirit. As His vessel, Kathryn Kuhlman instilled God's hope and healing promises into those willing to trust Jesus.

It is my prayer that her words will instill that same hope in you. I have edited her words most sparsely so that you can receive the full impact of what God spoke through her. We have amplified her words with devotional materials that summarize various teachings she gave over the decades of her ministry. Read each Scripture as well as Kathryn's words and prayers as a daily source of healing words.

I would like to thank Dr. Ralph Wilkerson; my publisher, Tom Freiling; Steve and Joy Strang at Strang Communications; all the wonderful people at Creation House; Doris Laing, my mother-in-law, and Judi, my persevering wife for helping to make this project a reality. Most of all, I thank my first love, Jesus Christ, for using Kathryn Kuhlman to touch my life and scores of others with healing words.

Larry Keefauver, D.Min.
Editor

Faith Is More Than Belief

by Kathryn Kuhlman
(from the October/November 1975 issue of
Charisma magazine)

OUR EMOTIONS AND DESIRES are often mistaken for faith, and it is so easy to blame God when there are no results from something that has been purely of the mind and not of the heart.

One of the most difficult things in the world is to realize that faith can be received only as it is imparted to the heart by God Himself.

It cannot be manufactured. No matter how much we nurture and cultivate that spirit the world interprets as faith, it will never grow into the type of faith that was introduced by Jesus.

When we come to our salvation, it is still a matter of faith and, again, He gives us His faith to believe. "As many as received Him to them gave He power to become the sons of God, even to them which believe on His name."

The same Holy Spirit who convicts the sinner of his sin and sees to it that he is given enough conviction to convince him of his sin, will provide faith enough to convince him of his salvation.

But no man in himself possesses that faith. It is given him by the same One who gives the faith for our physical healing: the Author and Finisher of our faith—Christ Jesus!

With Him there is no struggle!

How often in a miracle service I have seen conscientious people struggling, straining, demanding that God give them the healing for their body, and yet there was no answer.

We can believe in healing! We can believe in our Lord and His power to heal. But only Jesus can work the work that will lift us to the mountain peaks of victory. We have made faith a product of a finite mind when all of the other gifts of the Spirit we have attributed to God.

To many people, however, faith is still their own ability to believe a truth and is merely based on their struggles and their ability to drive away doubt and unbelief through a process of continued affirmations. There is belief in faith, but faith is more than belief.

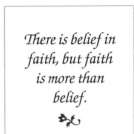

There is belief in faith, but faith is more than belief.

Faith is a gift. Jesus is our faith, and the Giver of every good and perfect gift is the Author and Finisher of our faith.

Active faith is unquestioning belief, trust, and reliance upon God with all confidence. Faith can become as real as any of our senses.

When we receive His faith we also receive understanding. Everything that God has for His children He puts within the reach of faith, then He turns around and gives them the faith to appropriate the gift.

Then Jesus spoke. With Him there is no struggle and the waves of doubt and anxiety and worry all fade away and a glorious and marvelous calm and peace enter into the heart and mind of the one who has received that which only He can give.

The only noise will be that of praise and adoration from the lips of the one who has just been healed by the Great Physician.

Day 1

Assurance

Let us draw near with a true heart in full assurance of faith, having our hearts sprinkled from an evil conscience, and our bodies washed with pure water. Let us hold fast the profession of our faith without wavering; (for he is faithful that promised).

—HEBREWS 10:22–23

I GOT UP EARLY ONE MORNING and drove from Kansas City to Concordia, Missouri, where I was born. I went back to that little Methodist church I attended as a child and was so shocked that it had gotten so small in such a short time. When I was young it looked so big.

> *There's never been a split second that I ever doubted my salvation.*
>
> ❧

When I returned the same pews were there. They were just as shiny as the Sunday morning when, at the age of fourteen, I received that wonderful spiritual experience of being born again. There's never been a split second that I ever doubted my salvation.

That tiny Methodist church seated no more than one hundred people. Perhaps you could have squeezed one hundred twenty-five into it. Walking into that little vestibule, I saw the rope that always rang the bell when someone died in Concordia. The bell was still there. It had tolled for so many people over the years. If a young person had died they would toll it once. When a middle-aged person died it rang twice. If an elderly person died they would toll that bell three times. Then everyone in town would run to the telephone to ring the one telephone operator and ask who had died.

I walked in and sat down in the same pew—

third row from the front—that I had sat in that Sunday morning. I was only fourteen years of age that particular Sunday morning when I felt the power of the Holy Spirit. I didn't know anything about the Third Person of the Trinity—nothing. I don't even remember who the preacher was that morning. I can't remember one thing that he said.

I had never seen anyone accept Christ as Savior in that Methodist church. I'm not sure that anyone was converted before me. But suddenly they were singing the last hymn. Holding the Methodist hymnal, I began to shake. Years later I recognized that the shaking was the power of the Holy Spirit on me. I laid the hymnal down on the pew. I knew I had to do something.

I did the only thing I knew to do. I slipped out from that pew and sat down on the front pew of the church. No one knew what to do with me. The preacher didn't know. I just sat there and cried for joy. One sister came up to me and said, "Oh, Kathryn, don't cry." I didn't have a handkerchief. My tears were running down my face. My nose was running. The sister who had spoken to me gave me her handkerchief and said,

"Kathryn, you've been such a good girl all your life; don't cry." Both of us knew she was lying.

Bad things didn't just happen to me in Concordia—I made them happen. But without any interference on my part, God intervened in my life with this glorious experience of being born again.

If you have any doubt of your salvation, receive Jesus as your Lord and Savior right now.

৯০

> *Lord Jesus, forgive my sins. I confess You to be the Christ, the Son of the living God, and I receive You as my Lord and Savior. Thank You for washing my sins away with Your blood and for giving me the gift of Your Holy Spirit. Amen.*

Day 2

The Prodigal Father

*I say unto you, that likewise joy shall be in
heaven over one sinner that repenteth, more
than over ninety and nine just persons, which
need no repentance.*

—LUKE 15:7

IT WAS FATHER'S DAY many years ago in
Youngstown, Ohio. At one service, the platform was filled with a men's chorus. During the
service, I paused and looked out across the room
to the junior ushers. They were all young lads,

none over twelve years of age.

So I just paused. Looking at these nice young lads I said, "Come up on the stage, and I want the father of every one of these young lads to come and stand with his son."

> *And they said, "Believe on the Lord Jesus Christ, and thou shalt be saved, and thy house."*
> *—Acts 16:31*
>
> ❧

The fathers came with their sons. Some were on stage in the men's chorus and others came from the audience. But two young brothers stood there all alone. No father was standing behind them.

I turned to them and said, "Where is your dad?"

One of them pointed out into the audience and said, "Someplace out there."

"Go and get him," I said.

So the two young lads went out looking for their father. When they came back, they said, "We can't find him."

I said, "Call him. Maybe he is in the audience and you don't see him."

One of those brothers stood there calling his

father, but the father didn't respond. It was so sad. They were the only two young lads standing there without a father standing with them on Father's Day.

On Wednesday of the next week, I received a letter written by the father of those two brothers. He wrote:

> *Kathryn Kuhlman,*
>
> *When my two sons came out looking for me, I got scared and ran. I left the auditorium and went to the car. I sat in my car the rest of the service.*
>
> *When the service was over, my wife, sons, and I went all the way home together without saying a word to each other about the incident on the platform.*
>
> *I haven't slept a wink. I can't eat. I have no appetite. And if next Sunday, you give an altar call, I want you to know I'll be the first one at the altar.*

The next Sunday after the congregational song had been sung, I stopped before ever preaching a sermon and said, "Is that dad of the two young sons who stood alone last Sunday here? If he is here, will he please come forward?" That man squared his shoulders and walked down that aisle.

That day he made Jesus his Savior. Years later I had the privilege of speaking at Oral Roberts University for the graduation of those two young men.

That father's homecoming to Jesus conveyed a blessing on his children that impacted them for the rest of their lives.

> *Your decision to accept Jesus today affects your household—your children and your children's children.*
>
> ❧

Your decision to accept Jesus today affects your household—your children and your children's children. Accept Jesus as Lord and Savior and break every curse and bondage from the past in His precious name.

❧

Jesus, I accept You as my Lord and Savior. Help me to be there as Your light and witness for my children and my children's children. Amen.

Day 3

The Apple of His Eye

Keep me as the apple of the eye,
hide me under the shadow of thy wings.

—Psalm 17:8

My papa never went to church. He hated preachers. If he saw the preacher coming down the street and the preacher didn't see him, he would duck out of sight. The preacher would never see him.

Papa only went to church at Christmastime when his girl would give a recitation or on children's day when she sang a song. They always said that Kathryn was the apple of her papa's eye. And I knew it.

Yes, Kathryn, that mean little girl with her freckled face and red hair, was the apple of her papa's eye. I knew it, and it was my security.

> I would say to Jesus, "I desire one thing above everything else in the world: to be the apple of Your eye."

Every time I stood up to give a recitation I only saw one person in that little church and that was Papa. I did my best for Papa. I was the apple of his eye.

Over the years, I had one verse of Scripture that I would weep over. I held it closely to me. It's been the motivating force of my life. "Keep me as the apple of the eye, hide me under . . . thy wings." A million times I held this precious Word in my heart. I knew the security that there was in being the apple of *His* eye.

You know, my papa never laid a hand on me—

never. All Papa had to do was to look at me in a certain way, that's all. If I disappointed him, he'd just look at me in a certain way, that's all. And I loved him so much. I was the apple of his eye, and I wasn't going to let him down.

I would say to Jesus, "I live for only one thing. Just one thing. That's all. I desire one thing above everything else in the world: to be the apple of Your eye. I want Your smile. I want Your favor. I want Your love. Nobody in the world knows how weary I get in body. But it's all worth it to be the apple of Your eye."

No matter what we have done, He loves us. We are unique and special in His sight. As sons and daughters, we can call God *Abba, Father,* which means *Papa.* We are always the apple of His eye.

❦

Abba, Father, I thank You that
I am the apple of Your eye.
Abba, I always desire to please
You. Amen.

Day 4

God's Mercy

Let us therefore come boldly unto the throne of grace, that we may obtain mercy, and find grace to help in time of need.

—HEBREWS 4:16

OH THE MERCY, THE MERCY of our Lord Jesus Christ! May you get a picture of the mercy, the mercy, the mercy of our Lord Jesus and the grace!

God's healing mercy should be happening in every church today.

Do you know what God is really like? He's bigger than man's theology. We get so full of theology.

Theology is the human endeavor of studying God. Theology may profit some, but human understanding only grasps the finite.

God's nature is infinite. So is His mercy! His mercies are new every morning. God says:

> For my thoughts are not your thoughts, neither are your ways my ways, saith the Lord. For as the heavens are higher than the earth, so are my ways higher than your ways, and my thoughts than your thoughts (Isaiah 55:8–9).

Before the mind can understand, the heart must experience God's mercy, deliverance, salvation, and healing. Studying God brings our minds to theological reflection. Knowing God brings our hearts to embracing His mercy.

Theology inspires curiosity. I have so many curious people attending the crusades. They are curious about me. But I want them to be curious about God. More than that, I want them to meet and know God and His mercy in Jesus.

Mercy invites relationship. In His mercy, you can discover His healing love and power through a saving, personal relationship with Christ Jesus.

> *Studying God brings our minds to theological reflection. Knowing God brings our hearts to embracing His mercy.*
>
> ❧

❧

O Lord, have mercy on me that I might receive Thy healing touch in my life. Amen.

Day 5

Love Him ... Live His Will

Jesus said unto him, Thou shalt love the Lord thy God with all thy heart, and with all thy soul, and with all thy mind . . . Thou shalt love thy neighbour as thyself. On these two commandments hang all the law and the prophets.

—MATTHEW 22:37–40

REMEMBER THIS: DOCTRINE will mean nothing to you. . . . The greatest sermons in the world will mean nothing to you. . . . The greatest spiritual experience will mean nothing to you. . . . Unless you love Him enough.

God's plan is inside of you. It's within your heart. I believe God has a perfect plan for every life. No one can convince me differently.

- As surely as God had a perfect plan for Abraham. . .
- As surely as God had a perfect plan for Moses. . .
- As surely as God had a perfect plan for Paul. . .

So surely God has a perfect plan for the life of every individual. God holds the blueprint for each person's life.

> *There can't be two wills when you are living in the perfect will of God. There must be one will— His will.*

Life is important. I know that in this day and age, life has become so cheap. It *isn't* in the sight of God. An individual life is the most important thing to Him in the world.

Your life as an individual is important to God—vitally important. You can choose to live absolutely contrary to the blueprint God has for your life. Or you can take your life into your own hands. You can live life contrary to the will of God if you wish.

My life is ended, but yours is just beginning. Listen to the advice of a dear friend: "Never get out of the will of God."

> *No man can serve two masters: for either he will hate the one, and love the other; or else he will hold to the one, and despise the other. Ye cannot serve God and mammon.*
> *—Matthew 6:24*

There'll be a price to pay in living your life according to His perfect will. There can't be two wills when you are living in the perfect will of God. There must be one will—His will.

Two wills existed that day before Calvary. Jesus' will was set apart from the will of the Father. The price for your salvation could not have been paid in full until Jesus yielded His will to the Father.

Surrender is the price we must pay to live in His will.

His prayer must become yours: "Not my will but Thine be done."

Pray the following prayer as you surrender to His perfect will and plan for your life:

ॐ

> *Lord Jesus, may my prayer be the same as Yours: Lord, Your will, not mine, be done. Amen.*

Day 6

In Love, Follow Christ

I am crucified with Christ: nevertheless I live; yet
not I, but Christ liveth in me: and the life which
I now live in the flesh I live by the faith of the Son
of God, who loved me, and gave himself for me.

—GALATIANS 2:20

THERE MUST BE A DEATH TO SELF. That's the hardest thing in the world. Jesus said we must put new wine—the Holy Spirit—into new wineskins. The Pharisees and religious leaders of His day knew the letter of the law. They were well educated, but they could not accept Christ and receive the Holy Spirit because of pride.

> *If ye love me, keep my commandments.*
> —John 14:15

My mind is closed to everything else but what's in the Word of God.

Jesus chose the most unlikely people of His day to follow Him—common people, tax collectors, and fishermen. He was looking for people who were pliable, yielded material. Education doesn't make you yielded. Psychology and religion do not make you pliable. Dying to self and becoming alive to His Word makes you a pliable, usable vessel of the Holy Spirit.

When Abraham and Isaac went alone to the mountain of sacrifice, whom did God ask to die that day? It was not Isaac. Abraham was the one who died on that day—not Isaac. The secret of it all is loving Him enough to die to self and follow Him.

You don't obey His Word out of duty. You don't surrender your will to His out of force. You love Him so much that nothing is a sacrifice—not even self.

Live to please Him. In living to please Him, you surrender your will to His. In surrendering your will to the will of the Father, the Holy Spirit comes. That's what I've done. That is the key.

> *You love Him so much that nothing is a sacrifice—not even self.*
> ❧

You may talk about this wonderful power of the Third Person of the Trinity. It's glorious. It's the most wonderful thing in the world to feel this anointing and be led of the Spirit.

But it means that you follow. He leads—and you follow Him. It's so easy and thrilling to learn to follow Him when you love Him.

❧

Christ, I die to self that I might live to follow You. Amen.

Day 7

He Intercedes for You

Likewise the Spirit also helpeth our infirmities:
for we know not what we should pray for as we
ought: but the Spirit itself maketh intercession
for us with groanings which cannot be uttered
. . . he maketh intercession for the saints
according to the will of God.

—ROMANS 8:26–27

WHEN YOU COME TO THE PLACE where you seek His perfect will, and you do not know how to pray, then just be quiet.

Be still. Do nothing. Wait.

As you are waiting, yielded to Him, you cannot miss His perfect will.

> *You can't miss God when the Spirit is praying in and through you.*
>
> ✎

The Holy Spirit, who knows the perfect will of God and sees the marvelous blueprint that God has for you, will make intercession for you.

You have the great High Priest, the very living God, interceding for you. You can't miss God when the Spirit is praying in and through you.

So yield yourself to Him. Give Him your will and your voice, your tongue in prayer. Your all—give it to Him.

The Holy Spirit takes what you yield and like a potter shapes it into something usable and wonderful. The Holy Spirit will guide you. He'll intercede for you. He'll keep you under the shadow of His wings.

✎

> *Jesus, I know not what to pray.*
> *Intercede for me. Through Your*
> *Holy Spirit, pray through me.*
> *Amen.*

Day 8

When I See Jesus

*And the King shall answer and say unto them,
Verily I say unto you, Inasmuch as ye have done
it unto one of the least of these my brethren, ye
have done it unto me.*

—MATTHEW 25:40

HAVE OFTEN WONDERED what I will say when I
see Jesus face-to-face. I've often wondered . . .

I've never looked upon His face, yet I can tell
you what He looks like. I can tell you exactly
what His hands are like. No artist's brush has ever

done justice in trying to paint the picture of the One whom I love more than life itself.

Yet I've never seen Him. I do know one thing I will say when I see Him and look into His beautiful face. Just two words I will say to Him: "I tried."

Not to justify myself, understand. His blood justifies me through faith. I simply want to say to Him, "With my every ounce of strength and will, I gave all to You, my precious Lord. *I tried.*"

> *Therefore, my beloved brethren, be ye stedfast, unmoveable, always abounding in the work of the Lord, forasmuch as ye know that your labour is not in vain in the Lord.*
> *—1 Corinthians 15:58*

Until that moment, He will keep me as the apple of His eye and hide me under the shadow of His wings. Knowing I've tried my best, He does the rest.

❧

Lord, I know that to whom much is given, much is required. Grant me the strength to try all that You would have me do for the sake of Your glory. Amen.

Day 9

The Power of
the Master's Touch

*And whithersoever he [Jesus] entered, into
villages, or cities, or country, they laid the sick
in the streets, and besought him that they might
touch if it were but the border of his garment:
and as many as touched him were made whole.*

—MARK 6:56

THERE IS SOMETHING FAR GREATER than the
healing of sick bodies. I know it is wonderful to see sick bodies healed instantly by God's
power, but there is something far greater.

Jesus says, "You must be born again." It is not

optional. He'll never force salvation on you. He'll never force Himself on any man or woman. You come to Him because you want to come. The Scripture says, "Him that cometh to me I will in no wise cast out" (John 6:37).

I pray that you will feel His glorious touch:

- the touch that gives everlasting life;
- the touch that forgives;
- the touch of power through which He does a mighty work in your life.

> *His touch has made us heirs and joint-heirs with Christ Jesus.*
>
> ❧

There is no touch in the universe like the touch of His nail-scarred hand. All who touch Him are made whole. All who touch Him discover that salvation, healing, deliverance, and power are in His touch. The Master's touch makes all things new.

Do you remember when the soldiers came to take Jesus? What happened? The moment they reached to touch Him, they all fell under His power. "As soon then as he had said unto them, I am he, they went backward, and fell to the ground" (John 18:6). Falling under the power is also part of the Master's touch.

Our bodies are still frail and subject to corruption. Our redemption will not be perfected until we stand in His glorious presence. Now we are redeemed from sin, passing from the bondage of sin to life. Now we are the children of God.

> *And Jesus, moved with compassion, put forth his hand, and touched him, and saith unto him, I will; be thou clean.*
> *—Mark 1:41*

It's glorious to fall under His power and feel His touch doing a marvelous work in our hearts. But the perfection of His touch on our lives will not be completed until we stand in His glorious presence, when this mortal will have put on immortality and this corruption will have been made incorruptible.

Our frail physical bodies are simply not geared for the fullness of His glory. So when the power of God touches us, we can just stand for so long—and then we fall under His power.

When His power touches you, you feel His

love. After you have felt His touch and experienced falling under His power, you are never the same again. His touch makes Him so personal. Falling under the power isn't what's important. It's His touch. His touch has made us heirs and joint-heirs with Christ Jesus.

It's as if He's holding you close to His heart. Whenever you are that close to Him, you never cease again to hunger for His touch on your life.

❧

Master, touch me that I might
be made whole. Touch me with
power. Hold me close in Your
love, Amen.

Day 10

Praise Him

*Enter into his gates with thanksgiving,
and into his courts with praise: be thankful
unto him, and bless his name.*

—Psalm 100:4

THERE IS LITERALLY A PLACE in Him where you stand and breathe in His matchless presence.

There, you are not asking Him for anything; there, you adore Jesus.

The key that unlocks the storehouse of glory is praise. We praise Jesus.

The Holy Spirit will always magnify, will always praise, will always glorify Jesus. He's the One deserving all praise. Don't let anything keep you from praising Him.

See the Lord high and lifted up. See Jesus.

> *We vow to give You, Lord Jesus, the praise for all that happens in this place of worship. We vow with our very lives to give You the glory. We vow to give You the praise. We want nothing, Lord Jesus, to inhibit our praise of You—not circumstances, not finances, not troubles, successes, or things.*

The Word says:

- He inhabits the praises of His people (Psalm 22:3).
- Praise Him all the day long (Psalm 35:28).
- Fix your heart on God. Sing and give

Him praise (Psalm 57:7).
- Praise Him in the congregation (Psalm 35:18).
- Praise Him with instruments (Psalm 150).
- Praise Him among the people and the nations (Psalm 108:3).
- Praise Him with all creation (Psalm 148).

When we praise Him, He inhabits our lives, our sanctuaries, and our homes. When we praise Him, life is filled with His goodness and grace.

> *Don't let anything keep you from praising Him.*
> ❧

Remember: Whatever inhibits your praise keeps His presence from inhabiting where you are.

❧

Lord, I praise You with everything that's in me. Praise the Lord! Amen.

Day 11

The Holy Spirit Gives of Himself

But ye shall receive power, after that the Holy Ghost is come upon you.

—ACTS 1:8

BELIEVE THAT THE HOLY SPIRIT is pleased to give of Himself. It's one thing to teach in the power of the Spirit. It's one thing to preach regarding the mighty Third Person of the Trinity. But it's quite another thing to see His power in action.

We cannot understand the moving of the Holy Spirit. You cannot analyze the Spirit's power just as you cannot analyze God. He moves as the wind. "The wind bloweth where it listeth, and thou hearest the sound thereof, but canst not tell from whence it cometh, and whither it goeth: so is every one that is born of the Spirit" (John 3:8). Even though we cannot understand everything about the Spirit, we do experience His presence and power just as we do the wind.

> *You cannot analyze the Spirit's power just as you cannot analyze God.*
> ❧

But He is so real. He is beyond our comprehension. When you have the presence of the Holy Spirit, you have everything. You don't need anything else.

People without the Spirit won't understand. They haven't caught the wonderful Holy Spirit. They simply won't understand how He works or who He is.

And when He touches me, I can go for a long time and not be conscious of another single person. I'm only conscious of His presence and of following Him. I am like a violin played by a master violinist.

It's like waves of glory almost lifting me out of my body. The Spirit touches the strings of my heart and plays beautiful music.

> *The Spirit touches the strings of my heart and plays beautiful music.*
>
> ❧

The Holy Spirit in our lives is resurrection power that sustains our bodies. My doctors told me that my physical body could not take the beatings of all the crusades. But the Holy Spirit sustains me with the power of God's life flowing through my veins.

❦

Jesus, send Your Holy Spirit that He may reveal You and manifest Your power in my life. Amen.

Day 12

That He May Increase and I May Decrease

He must increase, but I must decrease.

—JOHN 3:30

EFORE EVERY CRUSADE SERVICE, this is my prayer:

> *Wonderful Jesus,*
> *I pray that not one person*
> *shall see me. I pray that not one*

*person shall cross the threshold
of worship the same person as
when they entered. Amen.*

What I pray for others, I pray for myself because there is none more hungry for Jesus than I. Every atom of my being is crying out for more because there is so much more. I continually cry out to Jesus, "More!"

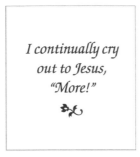

I continually cry out to Jesus, "More!"

The Lord knows my heart. I never plan too much in advance. I refuse to worry about the future. Jesus said, "Take therefore no thought for the morrow: for the morrow shall take thought for the things of itself" (Matthew 6:34). So I take one day and each service—one at a time.

When I awaken each day, my prayer is to know exactly what God wants me to do.

- How often do you make your plan and then ask God to bless it?
- How often do you awaken to your

agenda and not His?

- How much more of Him do you desire this day?

I want Him each day to increase in my life while I decrease. Are you praying the same way? When you die to yourself each morning when you awaken, He lives in and through you that day for His glory.

❧

Oh God, my cry to Thee is more of Thee, Lord. I hunger and thirst for You and You alone. Amen.

Day 13

Your Calling

Ye have not chosen me, but I have chosen you,
and ordained you, that ye should go and bring
forth fruit, and that your fruit should remain:
that whatsoever ye shall ask of the Father in my
name, he may give it to you.

—JOHN 15:16

Y OLDEST SISTER ONCE SAID to me, "You
know, Kathryn, I really still don't understand you." I would smile to those nearest to me
and say, "That's all right. I understand *you.*" The
person who knows me best is me. For a few

moments, let me tell you what Kathryn is really like.

You see what the world sees. It's just the glamour of it all. All that thousands of people really see of Kathryn Kuhlman is a woman gliding out on stage with a long, white dress. They see her smile and think that she is too theatrical.

Someone in the Shrine Auditorium who didn't know who my sister was, stood right behind her and said, "Don't you think she's (me) a little too theatrical?" My older sister turned around and said, "I want you to know that I've known her since she was born, and that's just Kathryn."

> *But if you've had a real call from God, no matter what the cost, do it!*
>
> ✦

Some may see the glamour of everything and think it's wonderful. They may think that mine must be a thrilling and glorious life. They suppose that all I have to do is get a long, white dress, stand up on the platform, and smile. On a talk show in Dallas, Texas, an interviewer asked me, "Miss Kuhlman, what would you say to a woman who aspires to be a woman preacher?"

Do you know what I said? My answer shocked the woman who was interviewing me, and she didn't get her breath the balance of the telecast. I said, "I'll tell you what to do. Don't do it! Don't do it! If you haven't already heard from God, don't do it! If you have never had a real call from God, don't enter ministry."

But if you've had a real call from God, no matter what the cost, do it! One not called can never find enough excuses for staying in ministry. One called can never find a way to leave. What is God's call on your life?

❧

Lord Jesus, only You can call and ordain me for whatever ministry You would have me do. Enable me to hear, know, and obey Your call. Amen.

Day 14

God Shall Supply My Need

If a son shall ask bread of any of you that is a father, will he give him a stone? . . . If ye then, being evil, know how to give good gifts unto your children: how much more shall your heavenly Father give the Holy Spirit to them that ask him?

—LUKE 11:11–13

I REMEMBER SOMETHING MY PAPA SAID when I was very young. If a girl ever worshiped her papa, I did mine. My papa was my hero, the most fantastic man who ever lived. I believed every word he said. Papa couldn't be wrong.

One day he said to me, "Baby, you know, you can have anything in the world that you want. I don't care what it is. You can be anything you want to be if you want it enough."

I believed every word Papa said. Papa couldn't lie. He worked hard with his hands. I was not a celebrity in Concordia, Missouri, but I was the daughter of the richest man in Lafayette County. So when he told me I could have *anything,* I knew he meant it.

He said, "Baby, you can have anything, if you'll work hard enough with your hands." For years, Papa worked hard and wanted money. He made a lot of money over the years. But Papa died without a copper cent. He lost it all before he died.

> *God always keeps His promises.*
> ❧

I have something I wouldn't part with for anything in the whole world. It's a dollar bill. I have it in a Bible. It's something very important to me. I seldom take it out to look at it, but there are times when I do take it out and look at it. That was the inheritance

I received when Papa's estate was settled. The man who was once considered the richest man in Lafayette County, Missouri, lost it all. He believed if you worked hard enough, you could have anything. Papa worked morning, noon, and night. But the man who would have given me *anything* only left me an inheritance of one dollar.

God's inheritance far exceeds Papa's or any man's. God always keeps His promises.

Human nature is fickle and uncertain. God never changes. The truth declares, "But my God shall supply all your need according to his riches in glory by Christ Jesus" (Philippians 4:19).

The inheritance that no man can guarantee to me has already been laid up for me in eternity by the God who meets my every need.

&

Almighty God, before I have a need, You know it. Thank You for the eternal inheritance in Christ Jesus. Amen.

Day 15

Out of Love for the Master

*And whatsoever ye do, do it heartily, as to the
Lord, and not unto men; Knowing that of the
Lord ye shall receive the reward of the inheri-
tance: for ye serve the Lord Christ.*

—COLOSSIANS 3:23–24

THERE IS ONLY ONE upon whose love you
can really rely and that's Jesus. My papa
loved me, and I loved him. But Papa died never
having heard me preach a sermon—never once.

Papa was killed instantly. It was almost as though my heart and love were buried with him. But I saw something.

One of the greatest experiences of my life was that my love for Papa was transformed into a much greater love. Love that one has for the Master goes beyond human love. It's something so precious, so wonderful.

The one thing I guard so carefully is this priceless jewel: my love for Him.

If I were to tell you the scripture that means more to me than any other, you might not believe it. "Keep me as the apple of the eye; hide me under the shadow of thy wings" (Psalm 17:8).

Nothing else really matters—not really. Under His wings, there is peace. When you love Him so much, you have eyes just for Him. Your mind thinks only of Him. Your purpose is fixed. You live just for Him. You breathe just for Him. You live to please Him.

Jesus has given me a lot of things that are so priceless. Yet I guard one thing as I would guard a jewel, the most expensive jewel in the world. The one thing I guard so carefully is this priceless jewel: my love for Him.

I seek to please no man or woman. I want His favor. I want His smile. I want Him to hold me close to His heart.

After every service, when the crowd is gone and I go back to an empty dressing room and take off my long, white dress, I think: *Did I please Him? Did I do my best for my heavenly Father?*

❧

Father, I love You as I love no other. I live to please You. All that I do, I do out of love for You. Amen.

Day 16

The Cost of Discipleship

*I beseech you . . . that ye present your bodies a
living sacrifice, holy, acceptable unto God . . .
And be not conformed to this world: but be
ye transformed by the renewing of your mind,
that ye may prove what is that good, and
acceptable, and perfect, will of God.*

—ROMANS 12:1–2

EVERYTHING WORTHWHILE costs something.
What do you want more than anything else?
What in life is it? Whatever it is, it will cost you.
Some know what their goals are and are willing

to pay the price to attain those goals. They will break hearts or ride over people to reach their goals. No matter what it costs—ethical or unethical—some are determined to get what they want. They pursue their goals without caring what they do to someone else.

But there's nothing that demands a higher price than being the apple of His eye and knowing that underneath are the everlasting arms. The cost involves one of two wills being surrendered. The cost of discipleship is surrendering your will to His will. It's the hardest thing in the world. He has a perfect will for you.

> *Surrender that will of yours. Surrender it!*
> ❧

In the shadow of the cross, Jesus had to decide the cost. He surrendered His will to the will of the Father.

Surrender that will of yours. Surrender it!

I cannot tell you that it's easy to surrender. I would like to take your face in my hands and say to you, "It isn't easy." Nevertheless, I plead with you. If I could, I would get down on my hands and knees and plead with you.

You may aspire to great things and say, "Look what I can be. Look at my potential. I can be the world's greatest." The crowd may applaud you. But it's so temporary. All is so empty when you realize how fickle people are and how short life is.

> *But be ye doers of the word, and not hearers only, deceiving your own selves . . . For as the body without the spirit is dead, so faith without works is dead also.*
> *—James 1:22; 2:26*

I have weighed it all. I made my choice. I chose His will over mine. I have chosen to surrender my body as a living sacrifice. I pray that you too will become a living and acceptable sacrifice unto Him, filled with the Holy Spirit, and led by the Spirit.

It's your choice!

Lord Jesus, I surrender all—my body, my mind, my will, and my affections to You. I surrender all. Amen.

Day 17

Blameless in His Sight

*Even as the testimony of Christ was confirmed
in you: So that ye come behind in no gift; waiting
for the coming of our Lord Jesus Christ: Who
shall also confirm you unto the end, that ye may
be blameless in the day of our Lord Jesus Christ.*

—1 CORINTHIANS 1:6–8

A S A SMALL CHILD I tried to surprise Mama
by doing all the wash for her one Monday
when she unexpectedly had to go to the hospital
to sit with a sick friend. I tried my best, but I

ruined the wash. I had boiled all the clothes, and Mama's favorite, expensive coat had shrunk to nothing. Some of her best things were ruined.

I shall never forget her face when she came home. To my surprise, she forced herself to say, "You did a good job."

But I ruined that wash, though not intentionally. God knows that I didn't do it intentionally. I did it out of ignorance.

When I think of God, I would never hurt Him intentionally. Sometimes I may have listened to other voices instead of His voice. But there was never a time when I didn't want Him to keep me as the apple of His eye.

> *Wherefore, beloved, seeing that ye look for such things, be diligent that ye may be found of him in peace, without spot, and blameless.*
> *—2 Peter 3:14*

One of these days I will have preached my last sermon. One of these days I will have prayed for the last person who comes into a miracle service. One of these days my heart will take its last beat. The world may call me a fool for having given my life for the One whom I have not seen.

> *Made holy by His Spirit, I shall stand blameless before God.*
>
> ✌

But in spite of my failures and my mistakes, I will stand before Him blameless. Christ shall present me before the Father as blameless—blameless not because of my reckless faith in Him or anything I have done. Rather I will stand blameless through the perfection and the righteousness of His only begotten Son, my Lord and Savior, who gave me His Spirit to make me holy, pure, and blameless. Made holy by His Spirit, I shall stand blameless before God.

❧

Wash me with Your blood, Lord Jesus, that I might be blameless and without spot in Your presence. Amen.

Day 18

Under His Wings

He that dwelleth in the secret place of the
most High shall abide under the shadow of the
Almighty. I will say of the Lord, He is my refuge
and my fortress: my God; in him will I trust . . .
He shall cover thee with his feathers, and under
his wings shalt thou trust: his truth shall
be thy shield and buckler.

—PSALM 91:1–4

O H, BELOVED, to be in a position of being completely hidden under His wings! It feels so secure.

There is such safety and refuge.
You will become a very secure person.
The only person really secure is the one
who knows that underneath are the
everlasting arms.
You are covered by His wings.

Covered by Thy wings,
I am protected.
I am not afraid.
I am no longer insecure.

Under Thy wings,
The evil one cannot touch me.
The waters shall not overflow.

As the apple of His eye,
I have been covered by His wings.
Lord God, cover me with Thy wings.

> *Lord God, cover me*
> *with Thy wings.*
> ❧

Hide me in the secret place, under the shadow of Thy wings. Amen. Only there am I secure and unafraid.

Day 19

The Baptism of the Holy Spirit

I indeed baptize you with water unto repentance: but he that cometh after me is mightier than I, whose shoes I am not worthy to bear: he shall baptize you with the Holy Ghost, and with fire.

—MATTHEW 3:11

WAS PREACHING THE GOSPEL in Joliet, Illinois. I was in my teens. I'll never forget a young lady, a teacher, who remained at the altar praying after everyone else had left.

She knew absolutely nothing about the Holy

Spirit or the baptism of the Holy Spirit. She had never heard anyone speak in an unknown tongue—never.

> For John truly baptized with water; but ye shall be baptized with the Holy Ghost not many days hence.
> —Acts 1:5

I took my place at the side of her mother. There were only three or four of us left in the room when suddenly it happened. She looked up, raised both hands, and began to sing the most beautiful song I have ever heard. Her voice was clear as a bell. That was a language so beautiful and wonderful. It was absolute perfection. I had never heard such singing.

Her mother, sitting there in the semidarkness, clasped my hands and said, "Kathryn, that's not my daughter. My daughter can't even carry a tune. That's not my daughter." We sat there awed. The glory of the Lord was on her face. She was beautiful.

Perhaps for fifteen minutes or more the perfection of that voice and the perfection of that music in an unknown language filled the room. I was seeing the Holy Spirit. I was witnessing something

I had never known before. I had seen the baptism of the Holy Spirit.

Always remember this: I believe in the baptism of the Holy Spirit with every atom of my being. There is an experience when He comes in and fills that vessel of yours that is absolutely perfect.

> *When the baptism of the Holy Spirit comes, it is absolute perfection.*
>
> ❧

A lot of things are called the baptism of the Holy Spirit which are not. It will not be babblings. When the baptism of the Holy Spirit comes, it is absolute perfection.

The Holy Spirit gives a perfect language. Everything we receive must come through Jesus. He is the One who gives the Holy Spirit, and He is the giver of the baptism of the Holy Spirit.

❧

Lord Jesus, baptize me with the Holy Spirit and with fire. Purge, cleanse, and purify me that Your perfect language might flow through me in worship and prayer. Amen.

Day 20

Hungry for More of the Holy Spirit

How is it then, brethren? when ye come
together, every one of you hath a psalm,
hath a doctrine, hath a tongue, hath a revela-
tion, hath an interpretation. Let all things be
done unto edifying.

—1 CORINTHIANS 14:26

SOMETIMES I THINK WE TURN to the mechanics of the Holy Spirit. We lose sight of the truth. In Portland, Oregon, a Catholic sister from the Monastery of the Precious Light was in a meeting. She had never seen anyone filled with the Holy Spirit.

She timidly came to the stage and said, "I've just been healed."

I said, "Oh, Sister, that is wonderful. I'm so glad."

Then she turned to go. She took no more than three steps before she turned to me again and timidly whispered, "I'm so hungry for more of the Holy Spirit."

> *Blessed are ye that hunger now: for ye shall be filled. Blessed are ye that weep now: for ye shall laugh.*
> *—Luke 6:21*

In that moment I did not pray for her. In that moment she was touched by the power of God and was lying prostrate under the power of God. Before she ever hit the floor, she began to speak in the most beautiful language. No one had told her the mechanics.

Remember something: Noise is not the sign of power. A holy hush came over that crowd. In that moment five thousand hearts beat as one and all that could be heard was the hush of those people—a holy hush. The angel bent low and that Catholic sister, who had never been taught how to speak, pray, or sing in tongues, surrendered herself to Him. The Holy Spirit was filling her, and suddenly her lips spoke a heavenly language.

It was so beautiful that you felt like taking off your shoes. We were standing on holy ground. We were standing in the presence of the Most High. The perfection of the Holy Spirit was there.

Do you hunger for more of His Spirit?

Do you thirst for His living water so that you are never satisfied, never completely filled? The Holy Spirit desires to fill, to baptize, to anoint, and to perfect you in Christ. Are you willing? Do you hunger for more of His Spirit?

Jesus, make of my tongue and life a tabernacle, a place of holy ground so that all I utter might be absolute perfection in Your sight. Amen.

Day 21

The Last Hour

And it shall come to pass in the last days, saith
God, I will pour out of my Spirit upon all flesh:
and your sons and your daughters shall prophesy,
and your young men shall see visions, and your
old men shall dream dreams.

—ACTS 2:17

BELIEVE IN THIS LAST HOUR, all the fruit, all the
gifts of the Holy Spirit are being restored to the
church. There were miracle services in the early
church where all were healed by the power of
God.

On the day of Pentecost, all in that upper room were filled with the Holy Ghost. That hour is at hand, my friend, when there will be times of such oneness in the Spirit that the Holy Ghost will come upon those in the assembly as at Pentecost.

Those who know absolutely nothing about the Holy Spirit will have great waves of glory come upon them, and every person present will be filled with the Holy Spirit.

Such a day of Pentecost is upon us in this last hour. I believe that the Spirit will come upon us in these last days in such power that everyone in a service will be healed, saved, delivered, and filled with the Holy Spirit.

If you are ready, are you praying in one accord for Pentecost?

In Acts 1:14 the early leaders of the church met together and continued in one accord in prayer. There is a secret in oneness in the Spirit. If your church is to experience Pentecost, then there must be oneness on your board and among your leadership. Because, you see, the Holy Spirit is easily grieved. I don't think any of us knows how really sensitive the Holy Spirit is.

> *And they were all filled with the Holy Ghost, and began to speak with other tongues, as the Spirit gave them utterance.*
> *—Acts 2:4*
>
> ❧

In that upper room they were all in one accord. The Holy Spirit did not descend until there was oneness. The Spirit works in oneness with the Father and the Son. So too, we must be one in the Spirit if we are ever to knows the power of Pentecost.

❧

Father, we pray for an out-pouring upon us in this last hour that we might experience Pentecost in our midst. I pray for oneness in the Spirit. Prepare me for Pentecost. Amen.

Day 22

Grieve Not the Holy Spirit

If there be therefore any consolation in Christ, if any comfort of love, if any fellowship of the Spirit, if any bowels and mercies, Fulfil ye my joy, that ye be likeminded, having the same love, being of one accord, of one mind. Let nothing be done through strife or vainglory.

—PHILIPPIANS 2:1–3

WHEN ONE IS LED it means that one follows. Whoever follows Christ will be in the right place to receive His power and blessings. There's not one thing that God has done for me that He won't do for you. God will use you just as He uses me. He'll give to you absolutely everything that He has given to me, if you will pay the price.

The price is not cheap. Everybody is out for a bargain these days, but God has no bargains.

> *Cast me not away from thy presence; and take not thy holy spirit from me.*
> —Psalm 51:11
>
> ❧

There's a price, and it depends on what you want most. I know what David meant when he cried out, "Take not Thy Holy Spirit from me." I am not afraid of Satan. I can use all the weapons that Jesus used. I simply speak God's Word, "It is written," and Satan is defeated. I have not one fear. I fear no man lest I grieve the Holy Spirit, lest His anointing should leave.

You may see only the glamour associated with doing ministry. You may want to do ministry, but it's not cheap. Thousands in the crusade arenas saw the miracles and the glory. But only a few of them saw the price that was paid before those miracles took place.

Take not Thy Holy Spirit from me.

God can take everything that I have. I'll live on bread and water for the rest of my life. I'll preach the gospel from the street corner, but *take not Thy Holy Spirit from me.*

If I knew the Holy Spirit would be parted from me, I would never again walk out on a stage. I would never go through a form of ministry or make a pretense. I couldn't live if I had anything less than what I have with the Holy Spirit. I wouldn't want to live. That fellowship that Paul was talking about in not grieving the Holy Spirit, I must have. Nothing else matters.

> *And grieve not the holy Spirit of God, whereby ye are sealed unto the day of redemption.*
> —*Ephesians 4:30*

How is your fellowship with the Holy Spirit? Are you avoiding at all cost grieving the Holy Spirit? Are you settling for less than all the Holy Spirit has for you? Grieve not the Holy Spirit.

Lord, take not Thy Holy Spirit from me. Order my steps in ministry so that I will never

grieve You. Make me so sensi-
tive to Thy leading that my
every action, word, and thought
will give You the glory. Amen.

Day 23

Having Nothing,
Yield Yourself to Him

*I count all things but loss for the excellency of
the knowledge of Christ Jesus my Lord: for
whom I have suffered the loss of all things, and
do count them but dung, that I may win Christ.*

—PHILIPPIANS 3:8

AFTER A SERVICE SOME ASK ME why I'm not weary in body? The answer is simple. Because I haven't done it. I love standing there watching the Holy Spirit.

I love preaching a positive gospel. It is not my

business to preach against things. I never preach sermons against smoking or drinking alcohol. When people meet Jesus, He will deliver them of all that's negative. So it's my business to lift up Jesus Christ. When He is lifted up, He draws all men unto Himself and they are transformed, becoming new creatures in Christ. I enjoy watching the Holy Spirit change lives.

He just asks for yielded vessels.

It's my privilege to see what the Holy Spirit is doing. I've watched Him empty wheelchairs. I thrill for the lame that walk. I rejoice when I see Him open deaf ears. I see Him deliver all those people in negative bondages. So why shouldn't I be refreshed? The positive gospel of Christ renews me.

I have nothing to do with it whatsoever. I haven't entered into the picture. When we do ministry in our own strength, we fall apart. If we spend our time and effort preaching against things, then we become emotionally drained and spent. Why? We are attacking things in our own strength instead of lifting Jesus up by the power of the Holy Spirit.

It's hard work when we do anything without the Holy Spirit. The thing is that He doesn't ask for golden vessels. He doesn't ask for silver vessels. He just asks for yielded vessels. That's the glory of it.

I have no talents. I was born without anything. Nothing! That's the reason it was easy for me to say, "Take nothing, and use it."

❧

Lord Jesus, I have nothing to give. I surrender myself. I yield myself totally to the work You would have me do. Amen.

Day 24

What Will You Do
With the Cross?

*For the preaching of the cross is to them that
perish foolishness; but unto us which are saved
it is the power of God.*

—1 Corinthians 1:18

F OR SOME, IT MAY BE HARD to die on the cross.
That cross is there. Without exception
everyone must come face-to-face with the cross.

When you face the cross, remember: The cross
is what you want most.

It may look hard to you now. It costs so much, but is there anything in life that you want more? Can anything else meet your need for forgiveness like the cross of Christ? What will you do with the cross? That's the defining question for your life.

> *And he that taketh not his cross, and followeth after me, is not worthy of me. He that findeth his life shall lose it: and he that loseth his life for my sake shall find it.*
> *—Matthew 10:38–39*

The question may seem foolish to you right now. Paul said, "The cross is foolishness to them that perish." If you do not wish to perish, you must come to the cross.

What you do with everything else is temporary. What you do with the cross is eternal!

Jesus, I take up the cross and follow You. I leave all else behind. I let go of the temporal and grasp the eternal. Amen.

Day 25

My Prayer

And the Lord said, Behold, there is a place by me,
and thou shalt stand upon a rock: And it shall
come to pass, while my glory passeth by, that I
will put thee in a cleft of the rock, and will cover
thee with my hand while I pass by: And I will
take away mine hand, and thou shalt see my
back parts: but my face shall not be seen.

—EXODUS 33:21–23

B EFORE EACH MEETING, I spend hours alone
with the Holy Spirit. He will not share His
glory with anyone, and I never want to touch His

glory. At the beginning of each meeting, this is my prayer:

> *Lord Jesus, we bow in delight. We are so careful to give You the praise. There's one thing You will not share with any individual. You will not share Your glory. You will not share the praise. We will be careful to give You all the glory. We bow with all of our lives before all of heaven. You will receive all glory for everything that is done in this place of worship.*

> *Jesus, trust us. We just want You to trust us. Amen.*

Day 26

Greater Works Than These

Verily, verily, I say unto you, He that believeth on me, the works that I do shall he do also; and greater works than these shall he do; because I go unto my Father. And whatsoever ye shall ask in my name, that will I do, that the Father may be glorified in the Son.

—JOHN 14:12–13

I F GOD CAN USE ME, He can use you if you will face the cross. I met a young Bolivian student at one of my services who knew nothing about the new birth experience. He knew nothing about the Holy Ghost. He had never read or taught the Word.

During the service, that Bolivian student was born again. A month later he was standing on a folding chair, preaching to an overflow crowd outside of my services. While he was telling this crowd in broken English how he had been saved a month before, the Holy Ghost fell and began healing people.

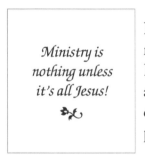

Ministry is nothing unless it's all Jesus!

God sent him back to Bolivia. Through his witness, the president of Bolivia was born again, and the wife of the president was healed by the power of the Holy Ghost.

That young man began an evangelistic, healing ministry in which he preached to thousands of people at a time in Bolivia.

If God can use him that way, He can use you if you'll face the cross of Jesus Christ and die to self.

Dying to the cross is a daily act. You die to Christ and live in Him constantly. It's a life of consecration. We must be absolutely dependent on Him with no crutch to lean on.

I know that I'm nothing. This young man was nothing until God used him. We do not have to be good preachers or wealthy supporters of the church. You see, when I received Jesus, I had nothing. So I have nothing to lose in following Jesus. And He took nothing and used me. Ministry is nothing unless it's all Jesus!

Pray this prayer:

୧ୈ

Lord, I am willing to face my cross and to die on it. More than anything else, I want Your Holy Spirit to use me. I want that more than life itself. Amen.

Day 27

Lonely, But Never Alone

Let your conversation be without covetousness;
and be content with such things as ye have: for
he [God] hath said, I will never leave thee, nor
forsake thee.

—HEBREWS 13:5

I HAVE EYES JUST FOR ONE—Jesus. I would lie to you if I told you that I wasn't a lonely person. Sometimes I feel like the loneliest person in the whole world. I'm surrounded by literally thousands and thousands of people. They press in to me. They crowd around me.

> *Out of favor with man, I feel lonely. But out of favor with God, I am truly alone.*
>
> ❧

But being surrounded by crowds is so empty. It's a great price to pay. So I cry out, "Keep me, Lord! I really love just One—You, Lord Jesus."

You may feel lonely, but you are never alone.

Your first and one love, Jesus, will be with you always. Never give up on Jesus. Rather, stay in the center of God's will for your life.

Out of favor with man, I feel lonely. But out of favor with God, I am truly alone.

Now when you do God's will it may not win you the favor of man. But stand firm. It's God's favor that you long for and cannot live without.

> *And, lo, I am with you always, even unto the end of the world.*
> *—Matthew 28:20*
>
> ❧

I never want to grieve His Spirit or have His anointing depart. I would rather die than have His Spirit leave.

So I always pray to stay in the center of His will even if I may feel lonely for a time. With Jesus, my first love, I am never alone.

❧

Lord Jesus, when I feel lonely, take me by the hand. Lift me up. On You—Christ—the solid Rock I stand. All other ground is sinking sand. Jesus, You are the One I love. Amen.

Day 28

The Power of God

Then he called his twelve disciples together, and gave them power and authority over all devils, and to cure diseases. And he sent them to preach the kingdom of God, and to heal the sick.

—Luke 9:1–2

I DO NOT BELIEVE I WAS God's first choice in this ministry, or even His second or third. What I do in this healing ministry is really a man's job.

But someplace men failed. I was just stupid enough to say, "Take nothing, and use it." And He's been doing that.

I think that in God's plan there are those, however, whom He calls for a definite work. For instance, I could not do the work of Billy Graham. I do not think that Billy Graham is called to do my work.

> *Whom God chooses for a certain ministry, God empowers to do that ministry.*
>
> ✕

I have been asked why Billy Graham doesn't pray for the sick in his services. Is it a lack of spirituality? A thousand times No! God called him to minister the way he ministers and has called me to minister in the way I minister.

I believe that God has chosen certain people for certain ministries. Whom God chooses for a certain ministry, God empowers to do that ministry.

But everyone can have just as much of the power of God. Every minister can have just as much of the power of God as I have if they will pay the price.

✿

Lord, empower me to fulfill the plan You have for me. Amen.

Day 29

Miracles

And they went forth, and preached every where,
the Lord working with them, and confirming
the word with signs following.

—MARK 16:20

I AM OVERWHELMED BY GOD AND HIS POWER. When I come out on stage, there is an anointing that comes on me, and it is very difficult to explain. I watch what the Holy Spirit is doing. He heals, not me.

These things are supernatural. That's the reason

it is so hard for the natural mind to comprehend. But there is an anointing that comes upon me. I am completely taken over by the Holy Spirit—just completely.

> *To see miracles you must pay the price of living a life consecrated in the Spirit.*
>
> ❧

But there is a price to pay. You cannot expect an anointing for four hours during a service if for twenty hours you have lived a different life than one totally consecrated to Him.

To see miracles you must pay the price of living a life consecrated in the Spirit. And He gives this wonderful anointing, but I still have nothing to do with these miracles. Learning to believe God to do miracles is so simple, even a child can believe in and see the miracles of God.

❧

Lord, I am Your child. Let Your miracles flow through me as Your willing, consecrated vessel so that Your anointing will touch and heal others. Amen.

Day 30

Faith and Healing

For to one is given by the Spirit the word of wisdom; to another the word of knowledge by the same Spirit; To another faith by the same Spirit; to another the gifts of healing by the same Spirit.

—1 CORINTHIANS 12:8–9

OUR EMOTIONS AND DESIRES are often mistaken for faith. Then it becomes so easy to blame God when there are no results from something that has been purely of the mind and not of God.

One of the most difficult things in the world is to realize that faith can be received only as it is imparted from the heart of God Himself.

No matter how much we nurture and cultivate that spirit the world interprets as faith, it will never grow into the type of faith that was introduced by Jesus.

When we come to our salvation, it is still a matter of faith, and again He gives us the faith to believe (John 1:12).

The same Holy Spirit who convicts the sinner of his sin and sees to it that he is given enough conviction to convince him of his sin, will provide faith enough to convince him of his salvation.

> *Faith cannot be manufactured— the Spirit imparts faith.*

Faith cannot be manufactured—the Spirit imparts faith. But no man in himself possesses that faith. It is given him by the same One who gives the faith for our physical healing: the Author and Finisher of our faith—Christ Jesus.

With Him there is no struggle. How often in a

miracle service I have seen conscientious people struggling, straining, demanding that God give them the healing for their body, and yet there was no answer.

We can believe in healing! We can believe in our Lord and His power to heal. But only Jesus can work the work that will lift us to the mountain peaks of victory. We have made faith a product of a finite mind when all of the other gifts of the Spirit we have attributed to God. Faith is a gift.

To many people, however, faith is still their own ability to believe a truth, and is merely based on their struggles and their ability to drive away doubt and unbelief through a process of continued affirmation. There is belief in faith, but faith is more than belief.

Jesus is our faith. So the Giver of every good and perfect gift is the Author and Finisher of our faith.

❧

Lord Jesus, give me the faith to trust You both as Savior and Healer. Amen.

Epilogue
by Stephen Strang,
founder of *Charisma* magazine

A FTER I GRADUATED from the University of Florida College of Journalism in 1973, I took a job as a newspaper reporter at *The Orlando Sentinel* which was then called the *Sentinel Star.* I covered the normal kinds of stories that cub reporters are assigned—the police beat, court cases, meetings at city hall or the county commission. Occasionally, however, I would get a chance to do a feature story for the Sunday magazine called *Florida Magazine.* I was always pitching them with ideas.

In early 1975 I discovered that Kathryn Kuhlman was going to have a crusade in St. Petersburg,

Florida. As a newspaper reporter, I knew there was a certain detached secular "objectivity" required for this kind of story. But as a Christian, I looked at Kathryn Kuhlman's healing ministry differently than most reporters would. I was able to sell my editor on the idea, and I made my plans to go.

On a bus bound for the crusade, I met a lady named Betty Davis. Her name was easy for me to remember because it was the same as the movie star. She was a Methodist and legally blind.

I arranged to interview Miss Kuhlman after the service. The service began with praise and worship, as usual. We sang several stanzas of "He Touched Me," which had become Kathryn Kuhlman's trademark song. Finally Miss Kuhlman came on stage in her flowing white robe, talking about the Holy Spirit.

As the service came to a climax, she began to have words of knowledge about healings. Betty Davis, from my bus, ran to the stage to testify of being healed of her blindness. There were many other testimonies of healings and miracles. I took copious notes while the photographer from the Sentinel snapped pictures.

My interview with Miss Kuhlman took place, standing up, after the service in a bare waiting room somewhere backstage. I had a small hand-held recorder and taped the interview. I remember that our voices bounced off the bare walls.

Miss Kuhlman gestured as she talked, much as she had during the service. Meanwhile, a muscular bodyguard with a scar on one cheek stood with his arms folded, apparently uncertain of what a reporter from a secular newspaper might say or do to Miss Kuhlman.

At one point I asked her who would carry on her ministry after she was gone. I recall that she was very abrupt in saying that no one would carry on her ministry because Jesus was going to come before she died.

That was in the spring of 1975, and the article in *Florida Magazine* ran that summer with her picture on the cover. The photographer took the picture from behind stage as her arms were spread wide while a spotlight silhouetted her and made her look like she had a halo. After the article ran, I sent her a copy, and she wrote to me, saying that it was one of the nicest pictures she had ever had taken, and that she liked the story.

Shortly after the article appeared in *Florida Magazine,* the first issue of *Charisma* magazine was published. It was a small church magazine with fewer than one thousand subscribers, although we printed ten thousand copies. When it came time for the second issue (October/November), I rewrote my *Florida Magazine* article with more of a focus for Christians using some photos that the Kathryn Kuhlman Foundation furnished to us and even a little "sidebar" written by Miss Kuhlman called "Faith Is More Than Belief" which has been included in this book.

On February 20, 1976, in a hospital in Tulsa, Oklahoma, Kathryn Kuhlman went to be with the Lord. A couple of months after she died the Kathryn Kuhlman Foundation asked a young Canadian named Benny Hinn to preach a memorial service for her. Benny had been tremendously impacted by her ministry and had attended several services in which she preached in Pittsburgh, but he never met her. There are some who say Benny picked up her mantle, and perhaps in some ways he did. But he was never really her successor. She had no successor.

Jamie Buckingham was the ghost-writer of several of Kathryn Kuhlman's books. After she died, he wrote a wonderfully honest biography called *Daughter of Destiny.* (I didn't know Jamie until 1978, two years after Miss Kuhlman died. He became my mentor and friend until his own death thirteen years later.) Jamie presented Kathryn Kuhlman in that book as one of the most anointed women of our generation, powerfully used by God. Yet she was flawed in some ways. Not flawed like a Shakespearean actor; just a real human being who had her own struggles and who honestly admitted her need of the Lord.

Interestingly, one of her flaws was her inability to be honest about her own age. Her radio programs described her as "the young woman with a message for America." Jamie said that she had fibbed about her age for so long, he wasn't sure even she knew how old she was. He tells an anecdote in *Daughter of Destiny* about how, as she was being wheeled into the hospital in Tulsa just days before her death, she gave the hospital emergency room admitting people the wrong age.

Less than a year before, in my interview with her, Miss Kuhlman had assured me that Jesus was going to come before she died. Jamie told me later that she must have known even then that she was dying.

What can we learn from this? I think that Kathryn Kuhlman's life is an example of someone who totally yielded to God and was mightily used by God. Yet she was very human with weaknesses. We all have weaknesses. Each of us can learn that God can use us—no matter what our past is or what our own strengths or weaknesses are.

We can also reflect on the fact that none of us are

going to live forever. Like Kathryn, none of us likes to think about our own death. But we need to realize that we will spend eternity with God . . . or separated forever from God. That should motivate us to be sure our hearts are right with Him.

We can also realize that if we want our own life's work to continue, we must have successors. Judging by Kathryn's brief comment to me, she didn't feel it necessary to have a successor. Yet as Oral Roberts once told me, "There is no success without a successor."

EDITOR'S NOTE: If you would like to read Stephen Strang's original article on Kathryn Kuhlman from the 1975 October/November issue of *Charisma* magazine, along with her sidebar titled "Faith Is More Than Belief," you can read it on the worldwide web at charismamag.com and the search engine by typing in the name Kathryn Kuhlman.

About Kathryn Kuhlman

KATHRYN JOHANNA KUHLMAN WAS BORN on May 9, 1907, to Joseph and Emma Kuhlman in Concordia, Missouri.

Kathryn became born again in the spring of 1921 in the Methodist Church of Concordia. A year later she joined her sister and brother-in-law, Myrtle and Everett Parrott, who introduced her to the Pentecostal movement. Together they traveled from coast to coast until Kathryn began her own evangelistic ministry in 1928. Ten years later she met Burroughs Waltrip, who divorced his wife to marry Kathryn.

It was during their eight years of marriage that Kathryn realized she would have to choose between her two loves—"Mister" (as she called Waltrip) or the Holy Spirit. She chose the Holy Spirit. As a result of this tumultuous period in her life, she learned the meaning of "dying to self." Leaving Waltrip didn't come without paying a price—the stigma every divorcing believer experiences. But God always restores those who seek Him.

On July 4, 1948, Kathryn held her first Pittsburgh miracle service at Carnegie Hall. It would prove to be a day celebrating not only America's independence but also a new-found freedom in the Holy Spirit and the rebirth of her ministry. God blessed her ministry so that in the next twenty years it circled the globe.

On February 20, 1976, Kathryn Kuhlman died of pulmonary hypertension. Her ministry had spanned a generation and touched thousands—if not millions—of lives. Kathryn Kuhlman was more than a faith healer; she was a bridge builder. People of different races, social statuses, and religious backgrounds came to hear her and left believing in miracles and in the power of the Holy Spirit.

❧

This devotional material was taken from videotape and audiotape messages by Kathryn Kuhlman. To learn more about this great woman of God, you may wish to refer to the following:

- *Kathryn Kuhlman Live!,* miracle service, Melodyland, 1969; videotape presented by Beyond Productions, Inc., P.O. Box 3000, Dana Point, CA 92629.

- Panel discussion with prominent physicians at Melodyland, audiotape.

- "Asking Questions You Would Like to Ask," pastor's panel at Melodyland, audiotape.

- *Graduation to Glory,* graduation address at Oral Roberts University, 1972; videotape presented by Beyond Productions, Inc.

- *Kathryn Kuhlman 1972 Teaching,* address to students at Oral Roberts University, 1972; videotape presented by Beyond Productions, Inc.

- *Just Jesus—Precious Memories of a Spirit-Led Life,* address to students at Oral Roberts University, 1974; videotape presented by Beyond Productions, Inc.

Charismatic Classics
VHS Videos

Kathryn Kuhlman Live
1969 Melodyland Miracle Service

Azusa Awakening
1906 Pentecostal revival taped on location, featuring three people who were present, plus three foremost authorities on Azusa. Musical Drama: Seymour played by Andre Crouch.

End Times
by author of Dake's Bible, Finis Dake.

Heroes in Healing
A docudrama on heroes of the faith such as:
- Aimee Semple McPherson
- Kathryn Kuhlman
- Charles Price
- Smith Wigglesworth
- John G. Lake

❧

Beyond Productions
P.O. Box 3000
Dana Point, CA 92629
1-800-468-4588
Fax: 714-493-7544